DRINKING
TO DISTRACTION

JENNA HOLLENSTEIN

ISBN: 978-1-4834-0511-7 (sc)
ISBN: 978-1-4834-0510-0 (e)

Because of the dynamic nature of the Internet, any web addresses or links contained in this book may have changed since publication and may no longer be valid. The views expressed in this work are solely those of the author and do not necessarily reflect the views of the publisher, and the publisher hereby disclaims any responsibility for them.

Any people depicted in stock imagery provided by Thinkstock are models, and such images are being used for illustrative purposes only. Certain stock imagery © Thinkstock.

Lulu Publishing Services rev. date: 12/11/2013

For Lily and Stella, that they always have confidence in their basic goodness, brilliance, and imperfection.

Contents

Preface

Most books about alcoholism are bumpy rides filled with one hilarious or harrowing escapade after another, all leading up to a moment of clarity at which point the author hits bottom and finds a higher power. Not this one.

I never drove or worked drunk and never injured myself or someone else as a result of alcohol. I never woke up next to a strange man, was fired, went bankrupt, or became homeless because of my drinking. My story is different.

Instead of a series of dramatic events, my decision to stop drinking was based on years of thoughts and observations, writing lists of pros and cons, and conversations with friends, family, and a wise therapist. Though it didn't cause me to spiral out of control, my drinking detracted from my life in subtler ways: missed opportunities, unaddressed fears, challenges not taken, relationships not cherished, and creativity unexplored. Though I never "hit bottom," I eventually realized that drinking was not enhancing my life: it was distracting me from it.

Acknowledgments

Thank you to my wonderful editors, Colleen Clemens, Jean Baker, and Guadalupe Tomic, for their comments and suggestions, and for not letting me gloss over the hard parts. To my mom Terry, my dad Peter, and sister Mel for urging me on, post by post and then page by page. To Andrea for his unfaltering support and love as we take life together one day at a time. To Edouard for proposing the radical concept that the consequences of being myself might not be so dire. And to Susan for introducing me to Shamatha practice and for becoming the gentle voice of sanity I now hear in my head.

Chapter 1

Sobering Thoughts

If I had to pick my lowest point, this would have been it.

In 2007, my first book was published. Writing it was a painful, plodding process that took much longer than necessary. This was largely because of my preconceptions about writing: I liked the idea of writing much more than the actual writing process, which required discipline and perseverance.

Because I also had a full-time job, I wrote the book during weekends. And by "write" I mean I alternated between setting unrealistic goals and outright procrastination. For example, I wouldn't write unless I had eight uninterrupted hours. On the rare occasion I did find such time, I spent the first two hours cleaning my apartment and the next two reviewing my research, clicking through web pages, and thumbing through journals, afraid to leave anything out.

After a solid four hours of *not writing*, I felt like a fraud. It was then that I rationalized having a glass of wine, reasoning that it would grease the finger joints and let the words flow out of me and onto the blank computer screen. This never happened. At best, drinking resulted in a few awkward sentences or in reworking the content I already wrote. At worst, I felt sleepy and unfocused, and wanted a second glass of wine. By that point, utterly disgusted with myself, I usually gave up and took a nap. The trifecta of unrealistic rules, procrastination, and perfectionism continued for months. It wasn't until I created a realistic schedule with small, achievable goals—and banished alcohol until the day's writing was done—that I was able to complete the book.

When it was finally published, some friends threw me a book party at a swanky restaurant in Boston's Back Bay. Though it was meant to be a surprise, I had a sneaking suspicion about their plans and fantasized about how it would go down. At first everything lived up to my expectations. The restaurant's bar was filled with the twenty or so friends who showed up to celebrate with me; my sister and her husband came from out of town. There were basil martinis and bottles of champagne. I felt special and admired.

The Sicilian scientist I was dating at the time—someone about whom I had both great hopes and a few troubling doubts—was nowhere to be found. I assumed he would arrive late, as he often did, because of commitments at the lab. But through every congratulation and conversation with the friends and loved ones who *were* there, my eyes were trained on the door of the restaurant, anxiously awaiting his arrival. When we could wait no longer, we moved the party from the bar to the dining room, and the chair beside me remained empty.

As the hours passed with no sign of him, I realized he wasn't coming, so I indulged my self-pity with one glass of wine after another. Each one took me farther and farther away from the people who were there, from my experience of this generous gift given to me by my friends, and from the pain of my disappointment. Alcohol numbed both my pain and my joy.

I recall the smiling faces of those there to fete my accomplishment, while I focused on the single missing person. I remember sitting in my chair and crying, hurt and embarrassed that my friends witnessed me being treated this way by someone I loved. I vaguely recall leaving the restaurant after running up an astronomical bill for my friends to settle so that I could continue drinking at a nearby bar.

What I don't remember is getting in a cab at the end of the night to go home. Paying the driver, walking up the steps to my condo, unlocking the door, and getting into bed—I know these things happened but they don't exist in my memory. That I left my laptop computer in the cab did not occur to me until the early hours of the next morning when I awoke with a blistering headache to leave for a business trip to Dallas.

Waiting in the United Airlines terminal at Logan airport, I held my cell phone to my throbbing head and listened to my boyfriend apologize. He had gotten the date wrong. He would make it up to me. It would never happen again. But as angry and disappointed as I felt toward him, a sobering thought occurred to me: I was the responsible party here. I chose to drink to the point of blacking out. I was the one who lost my computer. I alone caused myself this physical pain.

To the outside observer, I might have appeared just another young professional woman who enjoyed her drink and partied a little too hard one night. After all, nothing particularly unusual had happened. Yet my experience of the evening was one of shame and embarrassment at my erratic behavior, guilt for allowing my disappointment in my boyfriend to overshadow my gratitude to my friends, and fear at my ability to lose control.

Up until the night of my book party, I thought my drinking was under control. At times I felt like I was barely keeping it together, but before anything could happen, I reined in my alcohol use, at least temporarily. Though I had a handful of blackouts, no one else knew about them so they were easy to ignore. I never felt in peril. And there didn't seem to be any real ramifications to my drinking.

The night of the party, that perception changed. I lost my composure in full view of both friends and strangers. I revealed that alcohol had power over me. I put myself in danger and did something with real consequences. And all of these strongly indicated that my "controlled drinking" was coming apart at the seams.

Chapter 2

How Much Is Too Much?

It's a tricky thing to know when you've crossed the line from social drinking into problem drinking. For me, it usually began innocently enough: a cocktail with a friend after work or a glass of wine to unwind from the day. The first sip was the best. Or perhaps it was the anticipation of the first sip I loved most. Followed by the taste and the sensation of warmth that spread from my tongue to my throat and chest. About halfway through the first drink, I usually felt a wave of relaxation wash over my entire body—felt my muscles and jaw unclench. I equated the physical sensations of drinking with emotional release, the lifting of a burden. In clutching a glass, I sought to enhance the pleasures of celebration, connection, or relaxation, or to deflect uncomfortable feelings like anxiety, uncertainty, loneliness, and boredom. I wished to maintain the perfect feeling I had during that first drink and to remain there forever, but invariably I crossed the line. And once past my sweet spot, I continued to drink in an irrational attempt to regain it. I was never successful.

After drinking too much, I judged myself harshly. *Why didn't I stop at one? Didn't I see this coming? How many times do I have to make the same mistake before I learn?* But beneath these superficial judgments were stronger feelings of guilt and shame. I felt guilty for drinking rather than engaging in more productive activities like exercising, reading, writing, or really connecting with the people in my life. The money I spent on alcohol could have been better spent on my mortgage or saved for the future. Even alcohol's excess calories were a source of guilt. The shame associated with drinking ran deeper. I saw myself using alcohol as a crutch, a cowardly attempt to fill in the hours when I didn't know what else to do with myself—when I felt paralyzed by fear and uncertainty. I saw that drinking was allowing me to play it safe rather than to step outside my comfort zone and pursue a life less ordinary.

More and more, these feelings of guilt and shame loomed just under the surface but I was not yet ready to fully explore them. Rather than taking a break from alcohol to look honestly at my life, I tried every trick I could think of to keep alcohol in my life: drinking only on the weekends, drinking only in social situations, not drinking alone at home, eschewing hard liquor in favor of lighter options like wine, and limiting myself to two drinks regardless of the situation. None of these worked for long, but I felt as if the next moderation management technique was just around the corner, that the next thing I tried would allow me to drink in moderation, like a normal person.

Sometimes, when my drinking seemed to be getting out of control, I gave it up for a few days or a couple of weeks. Once, under the guise of following the South Beach diet, I stopped drinking for a full two weeks. During that time, I felt better physically and emotionally. I slept more soundly and had more energy. My mind felt clearer and I had fewer mood swings. My body felt lighter. But I missed the comfort of drinking. During this restrictive induction period, I fantasized not only about what carbohydrate-laden food I would first reintroduce to my diet but also about my first post-diet drink. I hoped that taking a break from alcohol would reset the behavior that was becoming ever more erratic. After the two weeks, however, rather than the single glass of Sauvignon Blanc I envisioned myself savoring slowly, I drained an entire bottle at home by myself. This vacillation between abstention and overdoing it began to happen more and more, as the pendulum of my drinking behavior swung violently between extremes.

Chapter 3

To Be or Not To Be

At some point, perhaps years before the night of my book party, alcohol and drinking began to occupy an increasing amount of my mental real estate. During the workday I eagerly anticipated cocktail hour. Or I perseverated over where to purchase a bottle of wine on my way home from work. Among my shopping criteria were selection, price range, and distance from my condo. But most importantly, how frequently or recently I had purchased from a certain place. I feared becoming recognized as a "regular" so I rotated my patronage accordingly.

Between work and home, there were several options for buying booze, but I favored the Best Cellars on Boylston Street and Bauer Wines & Spirits on Newbury. Best Cellars had the atmosphere of a coffee shop, with bright lights, eclectic music, and cheerful baristas eager to inform me about the viticulture and taste notes of their many options. There were always a few bottles open for sampling and the placed reeked of an innocent perkiness that never felt alcoholic in nature. Bauer was the more distinguished option, where the employees were informed and discreet. I could walk in, pet the store cat "Spooky," make a thoughtful selection, be complimented on said selection as I paid, and depart feeling as if I had just had a cultural experience rather than bought liquor.

I preferred to think of my alcohol-purchasing behavior as culturally savvy and was sensitive to the subtleties of less highbrow locations. I never patronized the Clarendon Wine Co., for example, because I had seen grizzled men slipping from there, furtively cradling paper bags in the crooks of their arms. Equally sketchy, but a reluctant favorite, was the Marlborough Market, a convenience store located a half-block from my condo. Though the selection was smaller, the Marlborough Market promised the shortest walk home with my prize. Still, I wondered if the people working there ever noticed how frequently I bought wine or liquor. Their poker faces never revealed whether they found it strange for a young, professional woman to purchase two nips of Tanqueray gin and perhaps a quart of milk for good measure. If they raised their eyebrows or exchanged knowing looks when I turned to leave, I never knew.

Once I had returned home with a bottle of wine, my preoccupation shifted to how I would limit my consumption. That I was thinking about the second glass before I finished the first did not bode well for my ability to control myself. Anticipation dissolved into guilt as I poured a second, third, and sometimes a fourth glass, emptying the bottle in a few hours. Those evenings of drinking at home alone usually consisted of trashy television, mindless online shopping, dozing off on the couch, and a few other fuzzy recollections. Mornings promised the spiky, sharp edges of remorse and my half-hearted resolutions not to repeat this scenario.

I Googled "Am I an alcoholic" and found a wealth of information including several questionnaires. One of the first I completed was the CAGE, a classic and simple test that includes the following four questions:

- Have you ever felt you should <u>C</u>UT DOWN on your drinking?
- Have people <u>A</u>NNOYED you by criticizing your drinking?
- Have you ever felt bad or <u>G</u>UILTY about your drinking?
- Have you ever had an <u>E</u>YE-OPENER (a drink first thing in the morning to steady your nerves or get rid of a hangover)?

After rapidly scanning the questions, I answered them silently to myself:

- YES
- YES!!!
- ABSOLUTELY!!!
- NO!!!

Clearly, I thought, *I'm not an alcoholic.* Weighing my negative response to the fourth question more heavily than my positive answers to the first three was a certain type of denial, to be sure, but also enough to convince me for the time being that my drinking wasn't that bad. The fact that I scored 75%—a grade I would have killed for in Advanced Placement Calculus—I chose to ignore.

There was more to this conclusion than mere denial. Basically everyone I knew would have answered the first three CAGE questions in the affirmative. Drinking was exceptionally normal, a regular experience for many of my friends and family members, most of whom were daily drinkers. At times we overdid it, but that didn't make us alcoholics.

I also found more detailed questionnaires from The National Council on Alcoholism and Drug Dependence, Alcoholics Anonymous, AlcoholScreening.org, and The Michigan Alcohol Screening Test, among others. A questionnaire by the Office of Health Care Programs at Johns Hopkins University Hospital comprised 20 questions, most of which were a definite *no* for me:

- Is drinking making your home life unhappy?
- Does your drinking make you careless of your family's welfare?
- Is drinking affecting your reputation?
- Do you turn to inferior companions and environments when drinking?
- Has your ambition decreased since drinking?
- Has your efficiency decreased since drinking?

- Do you lose time from work due to drinking?
- Have you had financial difficulties as a result of drinking?
- Is drinking jeopardizing your job or business?
- Do you want a drink the next morning?
- Has your physician ever treated you for drinking?
- Have you ever been to a hospital or institution on account of drinking?

These questions seemed to suggest a more obvious drinking problem to which I just couldn't relate. One of the questions I answered in the affirmative was clearly problematic:

- Have you ever had a loss of memory as a result of drinking?

But the remainder of the questions I answered positively seemed to exist in a gray area somewhere between normal social drinker and problem drinker; I found myself wondering who would not have answered yes to these questions, at least occasionally:

- Do you drink because you are shy with other people?
- Do you drink to escape from worries or trouble?
- Do you crave a drink at a definite time daily?
- Do you drink to build up your self-confidence?
- Does drinking cause you to have difficulty in sleeping?
- Have you ever felt remorse after drinking?
- Do you drink alone?

Answering yes to as few as three of these questions was said to be a "definite sign that your drinking patterns are harmful and considered alcohol dependent or alcoholic," warranting evaluation by a healthcare professional. I wondered whether the people who wrote these questionnaires were out of touch with reality or whether I was poking holes in anything that might suggest I had a drinking problem. Perhaps a little from column A and a little from column B? While I understood that each questionnaire was subjective, and that it was up to the individual to determine whether alcohol had become problematic, at the time it seemed I had only two options: Identify as an alcoholic and stop drinking, or not identify as an alcoholic and continue to drink unmodified. That I had additional options had not yet occurred to me.

Chapter 4

Not on the Same Page

When I wasn't Googling alcoholism questionnaires, I read a lot. Usually a fan of fiction, I was drawn to a new genre of narrative non-fiction: the alcoholism memoir. *Lit*, *Parched*, *Dry*, *Loaded*, *Smashed*, *Blackout Girl*, *A Drinking Life*, *Traveling Mercies*, *Let's Take the Long Way Home*.

I inhaled each story in a few nights and was held rapt by their tales of descent into alcoholism. Part of what made these stories so readable were the hijinks—from the hilarious to the horrific—brought on by alcohol abuse. Multiple-day benders, liquid breakfasts, drunken board meetings, ridiculous behavior, lost jobs, sexual escapades, drunk driving, cars wrapped around trees, mysterious bruises and gashes, emergency room visits, bankruptcy, drug use, prostitution, suicide attempts, homelessness, family rifts, broken relationships, rehab, and relapse.

Each was compelling, but none was the instruction manual I sought. In every book, I searched for but never quite found myself. There were glimpses of familiarity—looking forward to the next drink before finishing the one in front of me, a heightened awareness of everyone else's drinking behavior, unsuccessful attempts at cutting back—but the lack of high drama in my own story made me feel different from these authors. *They* were clearly alcoholics but what about me?

One memoir that resounded more than the others was *Drinking: A Love Story* by Caroline Knapp. With uncanny recall even when hammered, Knapp identified some of the more subtle and complicated issues surrounding drinking: how it was comfort and predictability that she sought in the bottle, the state of inertia in which she increasingly found herself in order to accommodate her drinking, that identifying as an alcoholic may not be the only reason to stop drinking, and that it could be possible to go without alcohol for a period of weeks or months (not necessarily forever) to assess whether life truly gets better or worse.

Three months before Knapp stopped drinking for good, she had a moment of clarity. She was drunk and horsing around with a friend's kids, carrying one of them on her back and one on her front, when she fell. Although the only person she injured was herself, she realized the potential havoc she could have wreaked on two small people that she loved. And while she appeared to be highly functioning in her professional and social life—and though she adored drinking as if it were a lover—she knew she had to make a change.

I too had these premonitions. Even though I had been spared regrettable sexual encounters, physical injury, and upheaval in my professional or family life, I suspected it was only a matter of time before my luck ran out. I was intensely aware that even a small shift in my fortune could lead to disaster: stepping off a curb into oncoming traffic, falling down a flight of stairs, slipping in the bathtub, missing a deadline, or date rape. What's more, I began to notice how much *I was not doing* because of my drinking. While I was aggressively having fun drinking cocktails in bars or snuggling up to a bottle of wine at home, I was not really connecting with the people in my life, was not deciding how to leave an unsatisfying job, and was not planning how to move toward a more satisfying life. Although my story didn't consist of raucous tales worthy of the beautifully bound alcoholism memoirs I read, more and more of my precious time was being drained by alcohol.

Almost always, alcoholism memoirs ended with the author hitting bottom, going to rehab, finding a higher power, and vowing to lead a life without alcohol, one day at a time. But what of that sober life? What happened after the drama ended? I searched for that next chapter but never found it.

Chapter 5

Four out of Five Friends Don't Think You Have a Drinking Problem

Little by little, I allowed my concerns about drinking to seep into conversations with friends. Settling in with a good friend to discuss dating, work, and family, inevitably the conversation made its way to my drinking. "Maybe I should take a closer look at my drinking?" was what I said, but what I meant was, "Do you think I drink too much?" (Note: this was usually said with a cocktail in hand.) The responses I received generally fell into two categories: "You don't drink too much; you just worry too much!" or "I give you a lot of credit for asking this difficult question. Now how about another round?"

Friends who didn't think I drank too much (A) didn't think I drank too much, (B) didn't know how much, how often, and why I drank, (C) were too uncomfortable with the concept of alcoholism to consider the possibility that one of their friends might have a drinking problem, or (D) felt that we drank about the same and didn't think they had a problem. Those who complimented my introspectiveness might have been a little more comfortable with the question. They might have even asked it of themselves at some point, and knew that it was something that was easier to ignore. I think they did give me credit for asking the question, and I took great solace in that for a while. But beyond that solace I knew that asking the same question again and again didn't bring me any closer to an answer.

Fortunately, I was working with a wise therapist during this time. He heard me voice concern over my drinking many times. At first he might have thought I was overreacting, but as it continued to come up in my sessions, he paid more attention. He asked me about my family history of alcoholism and about my experiences with depression. We talked about the difficult emotions I was dealing with and how I tended to medicate my discomfort with alcohol. Eventually he risked, "If you are so concerned about your drinking, maybe you should stop for four months and see how you feel?"

Four months? I thought. *Is he crazy? That is so long! How would I do it?* At first I didn't consider stopping drinking a real possibility, but that conversation stuck in my mind for a long time. It challenged me to move beyond the words, the questions, the intellectualizations and rationalizations. It challenged me to finally take some action.

Chapter 6

I Drink, Therefore I Am

While contemplating the possibility of removing alcohol from my life, I became acutely aware of how much I used it to define myself. For years, I had cultivated a persona that was interested in alcohol for cultural and scholarly reasons. I wrote my undergraduate thesis on the Mediterranean diet, in which red wine figures prominently. I dreamed of living that lifestyle, of drinking wine with every delectable, cardiovascularly healthful meal. I learned about viticulture—the various grapes and grape-growing regions, soil characteristics, fermentation processes—and the right food pairings. I thought that as long as I was drinking good wine, I couldn't have a drinking problem.

To friends, I was the girl who was always up for a drink. After work, before a movie, at art galleries, in airports and train stations, on planes and trains, at brunch, lunch, and dinner. I matched my drink to my mood and setting. I chose my beverage not only based on what I was eating, but where I wished to be and how I wished to feel. Champagne with oysters transported me to Paris. I chugged beers at sports bars and athletic events or with specific foods—Guinness with Irish food, Red Stripe with Jamaican. I drank whiskey to express my saltier side—Jamesons on the rocks or Maker's Mark Manhattans. And then there was my true love, gin. From Negronis, to dirty martinis, Tanqueray and tonic, and Sapphire straight up.

17

I loved the drinking culture, the community and camaraderie, the shapes and sounds of all things alcohol. Bars, bar stools, beer taps. The stout, classic stature of a cocktail shaker. The sophisticated Y of a martini glass, the roundness of a red wine bowl, the delicate flute meant for champagne, and the brandy snifter crafted to rest in the palm of your hand. The outline of each bottle communicated something different: the curvy elegance of a champagne bottle or the upright boldness of a cabernet. A champagne cork popping was my favorite sound, followed by the clinking of glasses and choruses of Cheers! Sante! Cent'anni! And I loved the taste. The mouth-puckering tartness of a Sauvignon Blanc or the cucumber crispness of Hendrick's gin.

Besides the sights, sounds, smells, and tastes, I loved how alcohol made me feel. When I was socializing, alcohol allowed me to feel less shy, awkward, and self-conscious. With a cocktail or glass of wine in hand, I could be dynamic, fun, and outgoing. Even when inside I felt scared and unsure of myself, alcohol helped me fit in and relax in otherwise anxiety-provoking situations like dating and work functions. At home alone, drinking was my constant companion, always there when I needed it. I could count on a bottle of wine to make me feel less alone. Drinking provided an escape from my pain.

Alcohol defined me in a way that other people might be defined by their career or favorite pastime. Scientist. Teacher. Marathon runner. Yogi. Nothing in my life was so prominent as to be my theme. Except for alcohol. It was the common thread that bound together the many disparate parts of my life—my field of study, my work, my interests, how I connected with people, and how I spent my time alone. Drinking tethered me in a way. Without it, I feared there would be no strong characteristic to weigh me down, that I would float away. Evaporate. Fade to beige.

And I worried about what everyone would think if I stopped drinking. Family, friends, and colleagues had come to expect it of me. Maybe my drinking was the part of me other people liked best. Without it, would they think I was boring? Would they think I had no self-control? That I was overreacting? That I had pretended to be something I wasn't? That I had fooled them? Maybe they would think I had other things to hide. Would my friends still want to be around me? Would my family ostracize me? Colleagues freeze me out? If I removed this important part of myself, what would remain?

Chapter 7

The Hard Questions About Alcohol

Up to that point, the only question I asked myself was whether or not I was an alcoholic. But since I could not answer that question definitively, I was unable to move forward. I realized it was time to try something different. That I was relying too heavily on things outside of myself to determine my future, and that none of these had led me to a satisfactory conclusion. Friends only saw part of the story; they were well meaning but didn't understand how much I worried about my alcohol use. The alcoholic memoirs I read were some of the more extreme examples—dramatic narratives that made for compelling reading—but not representative of the vast spectrum of problem drinking. And institutional alcoholism questionnaires focused on some of the more obvious signs and symptoms of alcoholism, but failed to help this individual navigate the subtleties of her own unique relationship with alcohol. I realized that no matter how many friends I talked to, how many alcoholism memoirs I read, or how many questionnaires I took, the solution I sought could only come from inside me.

I decided to take an honest look at my drinking and to consider the possibility that being an alcoholic was not the only reason to stop. I began by asking myself some of the subtle questions about why I drank. About the real purpose alcohol served in my life. About whether the persona I crafted around my drinking behavior was just that: craftiness—a way of making abusive behavior appear to be more functional than it really was. I started to explore what harm alcohol might be doing, even if not in overtly dangerous or dramatic ways. What I might be missing—both good and bad—by drinking my way through life. To this end, I came up with a list of questions.

Are there things I only do when I'm drinking? Because alcohol made me less self-conscious, I only went to parties, hung out in a group (even with friends or family), or danced if I was drinking. This didn't seem like the most dangerous (or abnormal) use of alcohol. But sometimes drinking caused me to act inappropriately. I might talk or laugh too loudly, horse around and embarrass myself, or say something stupid and perhaps even hurt someone's feelings. In essence, I wasn't being myself when I drank. Welcome sexual advances were difficult for me to respond to without alcohol, and initiating sex was impossible unless I had a couple of drinks on board. Without that liquid confidence, I couldn't take ownership of my sexuality or risk rejection. Sometimes I only expressed complicated emotions when I drank. When sober, I kept those feelings to myself, but alcohol loosened my tongue. It could also make me aggressive, however, so what might have been a heartfelt conversation could quickly escalate into an argument.

What feelings prompted me to drink? Drinking had become such a habit that I often didn't notice the feelings that preceded it. No matter the situation—positive, negative, or neutral—it always seemed the perfect time for a drink. But by looking more closely, I saw how I drank to grasp on to positive, happy feelings or to prolong or exaggerate celebration and relaxation. And how I drank to distance myself from fear, stress, anxiety, and sadness. I also drank to alleviate the monotony of boredom and the discomfort of loneliness. In most situations, I drank to manipulate my experience, to make it different than it was.

What would these emotions feel like without alcohol? It was difficult to imagine experiencing strong positive and negative emotions without an alcoholic accompaniment. I couldn't remember the last time I had done so. I imagined it would feel precarious. But at the same time, I was curious.

Did I need to drink to have fun? I couldn't remember the last time I had fun without drinking, but I did start to wonder about the real relationship between alcohol use and my ability to have fun. Did drinking actually make things more fun? Or had I just convinced myself that alcohol had to be present to have a good time? Did drinking make ordinary experiences seem more special? Or did it enable me to tolerate experiences I would not have enjoyed if I were sober? It bothered me to think I might be fooling myself into thinking I was having a good time, that I wasn't really experiencing things as they were.

Did I need to drink to relax? On vacation or at the end of a hard day at work, I relished a cocktail or glass or wine. Occasionally I did other things to relax; I went for walks and listened to music, took yoga classes, or sat in a coffee shop with a book or a friend. When I relaxed by drinking, I often overdid it by trying to attain a certain feeling and felt tired and remorseful afterward. When I relaxed in other ways, I felt more energized, like I was taking care of myself.

What is the quality of my interactions with people when I'm drinking compared to when I'm not? To be sure, drinking alleviated some of my social anxiety. After one drink, I felt a little more at ease with people in conversation, more capable of concentrating on them rather than on my own awkwardness. But after two or three, the quality of that interaction disintegrated. I had trouble paying attention, became sleepy, or was more likely to act out. If, on the other hand, I was chatting with a friend over coffee, I could sustain a more consistent connection because I wasn't thinking about my next drink or feeling the effects of alcohol on my brain.

Has my drinking kept me from doing anything? This was a difficult question to ask myself. Because I spent so much time either drinking or thinking about my drinking, I wasn't using that time to do other more satisfying or productive things. I wasn't figuring out what I really wanted in life, love, and career. After drifting from one unhappy relationship to another, I wasn't assessing my mistakes and determining how to move toward healthier behaviors. I wasn't deciding what I wanted professionally and planning how to leave a job that didn't meet those needs. I didn't even really know where I wanted to live. Though I had always wanted to move to New York City, I couldn't allow myself to consider that a real possibility. I had always wanted to do more writing, but I wasn't getting any closer to that goal. The realization that I was modulating my day-to-day experiences with alcohol rather than dealing with reality made me feel like a coward.

Thinking about quitting drinking felt as if my security blanket would be ripped from my arms. But in light of the answers to these hard questions, I could no longer ignore the possibility that alcohol was detracting from my life in subtle but important ways.

The reasons to stop drinking seemed to grow in number and importance compared with the reasons to continue. I was about to turn 33, in another dead-end relationship with an emotionally stunted mechanic/comedian/bodybuilder, and starting a new job the following month. There was no time to lose.

On my birthday, a long-time friend came to my condo bearing a bottle of red wine. He had seen me through my on-again off-again relationship with alcohol, from the birthday several years earlier when I apparently drank a jug of cheap Chianti all by myself, to the night I downed six Cosmopolitans and stumbled out onto the street, and the many times I stopped drinking only to start again.

I opened the bottle and poured a glass for him and one for me. I shared with him that this would be my last. That the following week I would be starting a four-week outpatient rehab program to help me bridge the gap between my drinking life and whatever came next.

The night before my rehab program started I sat home alone, fidgeting in my favorite big red chair. I hadn't had a drink since my birthday but I felt restless and uncomfortable in my own skin. I looked for something to distract myself from the discomfort—TV, food, computer—but nothing worked. Just sitting still was excruciating. I wanted something to take the edge off, but there was no alcohol in my condo. There was, however, enough marijuana for a joint, leftover from an appointment with my somewhat unconventional financial planner. I lit a match and inhaled deeply, feeling deeply disgusted with myself. *What has become of me,* I thought, *and to what else would I resort to avoid being alone with myself?* The next morning I woke up feeling numb.

Chapter 8

Going Down?

"Hi, my name is Jenna and I'm an alcoholic?" The first time I said those words, I tried not to let them sound like a question. "Hi, Jenna," the chorus responded. My outpatient rehab program lasted for four weeks, three nights a week, for three hours each night during the December holiday season. The first half of each session was spent having open discussion. The obligatory cigarette break served as intermission; I was one of the few who didn't smoke but went outside to participate in the ritual. The second half of the session was spent discussing how to stay sober during the holidays, one of the riskiest times for relapse. The ground rules for the program quickly became apparent: Speakers introduced themselves by first name only and whatever substance or substances had made life unmanageable. If someone was speaking, no one could interrupt, not even to offer support, and thanks were expressed when he or she was finished.

A sweet, middle-aged man, who arrived as ridiculously early as me and introduced himself first, shared that he would be kicked out of his halfway house if he didn't stay sober. A woman about my mom's age had become so committed to drinking that she left her home only to buy more booze; staying drunk had become her full-time job. An attractive and successful young banker cried that he couldn't count the number of times he cheated on his wife while using cocaine. I thought I'd found a kindred spirit in the articulate young man who wondered aloud whether or not he really needed to be there and questioned whether experimenting with various psychotropic drugs was inherently wrong. That was, until I learned that he had shot himself in the head during one of his drug-induced trips.

Over the course of the 12 sessions, I learned a lot more about the other people in the room. Each of them came to the program directly from an inpatient rehab program, the hospital, or jail. All were required to be there. Many had already been through this program or something similar to it but had relapsed, some multiple times. Several had lost their jobs, families, or homes. Some were on welfare or in subsidized housing as a result of their addictions. At times there seemed to be a competition between the participants regarding who had suffered more, who was worse off, who deserved to be there the most.

Toward the beginning of the program I didn't speak much; rather I sat quietly and listened. What seemed to be behind all of the tough talk was vulnerability and sadness—self-doubt, feeling unlovable. After a few sessions, I began to speak up. I empathized with the others and, despite our apparent differences, I saw only our common ground—feelings of inadequacy, the tendency to use a substance to alleviate suffering, the confusion of now trying to live life without that dependable anesthesia.

I got the sense that the others didn't think I belonged there because I had come of my own volition, and because I had a "high bottom." At first they tolerated me. When I spoke, I didn't get the same nods of understanding other speakers routinely received. A few times, when I was saying something, some of them turned away from me mid-sentence. Several times I heard someone say, "You don't understand," or "You're not an alcoholic," or "Maybe you'll get it in a few years." Our counselor reminded us all, "Alcoholism is like an elevator that only goes down, but you can get off at any floor." But in that room, there seemed to be no advantage to getting off the elevator earlier; there you had to have hit rock bottom, perhaps multiple times, to have any credibility. It occurred to me that it might have been easier if I'd had a more serious problem with alcohol, if something terrible had happened because of my drinking, so that it would be clearer that I needed to be there.

At the end of four weeks, the group parted ways. Some of the participants exchanged phone numbers and planned to stay in touch. All promised to attend regular 12-step meetings—90 meetings in the first 90 days of sobriety was the standard. Already having had such a difficult time convincing myself to quit drinking, I didn't want to expend any more energy convincing others I had a problem. I left with no phone numbers and no plans to attend AA.

Chapter 9

It's the Most Wonderful Time of the Year

That Christmas was my first sober holiday in more than a decade. Because I had secretly stopped (and resumed) drinking a few times before, my approach this time was to tell all my friends and family members that I quit drinking. This would allow them to hold me accountable, and my strong fear of judgment and failure would keep me in line. I expected questions and knew that people might not completely understand this decision. I tried to be open and honest about it without crossing the line into apologizing or self-deprecation. My mother's initial response was, "Are you sure you want to do this now? Don't you want to wait until after the New Year?" But once I explained to her that it would never be the perfect time to stop drinking, and she saw my resolve, she was supportive. As was just about everyone else. "Good for you," they all said. Perhaps it was the novelty of the so-called honeymoon period, but some of the early days felt almost easy. I felt cheered on by most of the people around me. Still I felt self-conscious and nervous about the impending holiday.

I spent Christmas Eve, as usual, with my family on Long Island. The house smelled of Mom's cooking. The tree was lit with strings of tiny white lights and decorated with ornaments collected over the past four decades. The bar was decked out too, with bottles of wine, gin, vodka, whiskey, scotch, tonic water, sodas, juices, and all the accoutrements—ice cubes, lemons, and limes. A cooler full of beer chilled nearby. My Dad's brother and his family arrived at five o'clock bearing the usual antipasto, eggplant parmigiano, and 24-pack of Budweiser. Mom greeted them at the door with "Merry Christmas," while Dad greeted them from the bar with "What can I get you to drink?" This was how he showed his guests that he loved them. He had thoughtfully stocked the makings for each person's favorite drink and displayed them proudly in anticipation of their arrival. He wasn't exactly sure what to do with me that year. I was a martini girl the previous Christmas and by this time of the day I would already have had at least one. Instead he mixed together some seltzer water with a splash of cranberry juice and a wedge of lime and handed it to me with all his heart.

The most stressful part of these family get-togethers was between the arrival of our guests and when we sat down to eat. During that precarious time, we stood in a circle around the kitchen island or sat on the otherwise-off-limits white couch in the living room and caught up with one another. In the kitchen, Mom avoided her own social anxiety by flitting between fridge, oven, and stove, plotting how she would deliver everything to the table simultaneously at piping hot temperatures.

Chatting with my cousins, Aunt, Uncle, and Nana, I felt guilty that so much time had passed since I had seen them. Mentally I admonished myself for not being a better cousin and niece. I should have stayed in touch, called my uncle on Father's Day, sent my cousins birthday cards, made it to the Fourth of July celebration. I always felt a little awkward around my family. I wasn't capable of small talk and tended to veer into topics that were outside of their interests. My sister and cousins were already getting married and having babies, while I remained the one most likely to get married and have kids last, if at all. Surrounded by people I was related to but couldn't really relate to, I felt anxious and uncomfortable in my own skin.

During Christmases past, this was when alcohol played an important role. That of normalizer. I assuaged my anxiety and guilt by sneaking off to the bar to fill a glass with wine or a less conspicuous combination of rum and Diet Coke. Any time my discomfort peaked, I scurried off and tamped it down with an alcoholic beverage. Returning to the conversation, armored by the drink in my hand, I felt a little more at ease. Until I didn't, and I repeated the sequence. During this evening, though, I did not give myself that option and made that clear to everyone who would listen. I still left the conversation at regular intervals but to fill my glass with only Diet Coke. Returning to the fray, I was still acutely aware of my discomfort and couldn't wait until it was time to eat.

Once we sat around the dining room table, I began to feel a little less anxious. I knew the rest of the evening would unfold in predictable fashion. First there were the bread and antipasti—olives, marinated artichoke hearts, roasted red peppers, and various meats and cheeses. The food distracted me from my shortcomings and I ate heartily, more heartily than usual. Antipasti were followed by the main courses, side dishes, vegetables, and salads. Then came the coffee, desserts, and after-dinner drinks. There were plates of picturesque Christmas cookies baked by neighbors and delivered to our door by their children. Mom's oatmeal-chocolate chip cookies. A birthday cake for Nana. After dessert, it was time to move into the living room to open gifts. Someone read 'Twas the Night Before Christmas per family tradition and we all laughed while my Dad took pictures. By that time it was getting late. My Uncle had to work the night shift. Everyone packed up their gifts and leftovers and bundled up to go out into the cold.

As my Dad finished the dishes and my mom and sister went up to bed, I sat in the dark of the living room watching the last embers glowing in the fireplace. I thought about making it through my first Christmas without drinking, about how good it felt to keep this promise to myself. And how even the most uncomfortable moments weren't all that bad. It seemed to be a matter of just outlasting the discomfort.

Chapter 10

Early Days

After surviving the Christmas festivities without relapse or family feud, I began the struggle of day-to-day life without alcohol. I left one job and was looking forward to beginning a new position early in the New Year, so I didn't have the distraction of work to help me pass the hours. I withdrew somewhat from many of my friends during this time because I wasn't ready to go to the same places—bars, restaurants, and holiday get-togethers—and not drink. While I tried to figure out how my post-alcohol life would look and feel, I immediately noticed an absence of guilt and shame about my drinking. Mornings were remarkably without remorse. And days weren't spent thinking about when I could have a drink, what it would be, where I would get it, and how I would control myself. Evenings were a different story—confusing and restless. I got through them by distracting myself with movies and TV shows, books, sleep, shopping, and eating. And by not keeping booze in the apartment.

Some physical changes became apparent in the three or four weeks after I stopped drinking. I was sleeping more soundly and woke up in the morning feeling refreshed. Though I usually didn't drink to the point of passing out, alcohol did interfere with getting a good night's sleep. After an evening of even moderate drinking, I often woke with a start at about three in the morning and had trouble dozing off again. Now, rather than needing to counter the previous night's alcohol intake with an equally strong amount of coffee, I could wake up with a single cup. (Though I still usually had two.) I didn't magically become a morning person, but I did feel more energetic when starting and going about the day.

Other signs of change were brighter looking skin and some initial weight loss. When I was drinking regularly, my eyes often looked puffy, my skin doughy, and my facial appearance seemed to fluctuate from day to day. These signs all but disappeared. My skin also broke out less (not surprising given the havoc alcohol wreaked on my hormone levels), and my skin tone evened out. I also noticed that my clothes fit more comfortably. Although I didn't weigh myself, I would estimate that I lost about ten pounds. This could have been because of less fluid retention caused by the seesawing effects of alcohol on body water, or the fact that I was less likely to mindlessly eat after a couple of drinks, or a simple subtraction of excess calories consumed as alcohol. It was as if my body was already celebrating my decision to quit drinking while my mind raced to catch up.

While I was sleeping better, I often dreamed about drinking. In one recurring dream, I raised a large martini glass to my lips in slow motion. I smelled the juniper aroma of the gin, saw the three large olives bobbing within, and watched as the beads of sweat rolled down the sides of the glass. But in the millisecond before I could take a sip, I caught myself, realized I had forgotten that I quit, and woke up feeling confused. Once the confusion wore off, I wished I could go back to that moment, to realize that I was only dreaming long enough to have that one cocktail.

Chapter 11

When Things Fall Apart

And then everything went wrong.

I started the new job I was looking forward to, but on my first day I realized I had made a huge mistake. Though my position was second only to the CEO, I was forced to punch in my arrival and departure on a time clock. My colleagues and I were bound to a windowless office with travel agency–style zero-privacy desks where we were instructed to keep conversation to a minimum, audible laughter was prohibited, and even the frequency of our bathroom visits was monitored. Based on the number of people fired during my first couple of weeks, it appeared that my new boss managed her employees the way Henry VIII managed his wives.

Outside of work, I was still dating the mechanic/comedian/ bodybuilder. He was supportive of my quitting drinking but three weeks into my new job—six weeks into sobriety—he went missing. Not flyer-on-telephone-pole missing, but *I left my phone in my car and was home sick for five days* "missing." Once he re-emerged, we patched things up for about three weeks before he broke up with me one Sunday morning. Right before Valentine's Day. In bed. I gathered my things, sat silently in the car as he drove me home, and never heard from him again.

Trapped in a new job I already hated, left without explanation by a boyfriend to whom I had grown accustomed even if the relationship was going nowhere, I felt I had finally hit rock bottom. My body felt heavy, unmovable, my mind confused and hopeless. At work I moved through the days in a fog, checking my email every 30 seconds for a message from my ex, trying to avoid the venom of my boss, and plotting my escape.

Outside of work I wanted nothing more than to disconnect from this pain. I shopped and slept and overate. I watched *Law & Order* reruns around the clock. I hunted for a new job online. And I talked to my therapist, my mom, and anyone who would listen. Though I tried to numb my uncomfortable feelings with these other distractions, my heart was broken. I would have loved to drown my sorrows in a bottle of wine, or three. But I knew that as soon as I picked up the first drink, I would be coming home to a bottle every night. That I would spend my evenings in a drunken, hazy stupor. And that my drinking might even become worse than it was before I quit because of my current situation and emotional state. Although I knew that alcohol might alleviate my suffering for a short while, it wouldn't change my situation. I had to do that myself.

So I closed the door to drinking. Did not give myself the option to go backward. During this time of confusion and uncertainty, my decision to not drink began to feel like the one thing I had any control over.

Chapter 12

Dressing to Distraction

With the extra time (and cash) I had from not buying alcohol, and a desire to escape my current situation, I often resorted to combing the racks at Filene's Basement, Marshall's, TJ Maxx, and even Barney's New York when there was a sale. I felt a thrill when I discovered a coveted label in my size, something I might never purchase at full price but when deeply discounted, I had to have. Even if the clothes I bought were outside my style comfort zone and didn't go with anything already in my closet, this sort of treasure hunt provided the satisfying distraction I was missing. As a result, I wound up with many beautiful but often unwearable clothes in my closet.

The pleasure associated with my new acquisitions was short-lived, however, and quickly gave way to feelings of guilt for accumulating an excess of unnecessary items and anxiety at the thought of my overflowing closet. Before I knew it, I was removing items to consign, donate, or discard. It went like that for some time: binge, purge, binge, purge. A vicious cycle.

My bargain hunting peaked when there were sales and any time I felt stressed, restless, or depressed. My desire to acquire reflected my need to fill in time, to pass the hours, and to not be left alone with my thoughts. Soon I recognized the pattern of my shopping behaviors—the feelings associated with these sprees and the resulting purge—for what they were: my innocent bargain hunting had assumed the position left vacant when I stopped drinking.

The nuances of my shopping habits even resembled my previous drinking habits. Whereas I used to fixate on Sauvignon Blancs, black flats might become my new obsession. While I used to chain-drink until a bottle of wine was empty, I would exhaust the style options of a particular blue jean company. Or if I had scored a Diane von Furstenberg wrap dress at Saks (Off) Fifth Avenue, I might hunt down a DVF chaser on eBay.

That my shopping habits had filled in for drinking was a mixed bag. Good in that it helped me to stay away from booze. Bad in the sense that it also masked the reasons why I resorted to these distractions. By quitting drinking, I felt I had taken an important step toward better understanding myself so I was frustrated by this resourceful, crafty side to my personality that sought other alternatives to dealing with reality.

Shortly after making this connection, I discovered The Great American Apparel Diet, an online community that invited individuals with a penchant for sartorial acquisition to abstain from all purchases for one year. I joined and vowed not to buy any clothing, not even the shoes, accessories, and underwear that fell into a loophole.

By removing shopping from my life for that period of time, I felt as if I was peeling away another layer of distractions from the onion of my identity. Without drinking and shopping to numb myself, I became more aware of the other distractions I had accumulated: overeating, oversleeping, zoning out in front of the computer, and binge-watching bad television. When a desire to disconnect from my feelings arose, I began to notice the triggers, to recognize the urge to anesthetize myself. And I tried not to immediately react or go for the instant gratification. Little by little, I practiced staying with the feelings, as uncomfortable as they were.

Chapter 13

Dating While Sober

After being dumped a few months earlier, I decided it was time to get back out there. While crafting my Match.com profile, I checked the box indicating that I didn't drink alcohol. Choosing to stop drinking while living in Boston, where booze was often the main course and not just a side dish, made dating an adventure. That is to say, an undertaking usually involving danger and unknown risks (according to Merriam Webster).

I approached the dating scene with some trepidation but also a sense of hopefulness. The past few months had revealed a different side of myself, one I was proud of. I felt courageous in my willingness to face my life without a buffer. And I was excited about the prospect of genuinely getting to know someone else. But it was not without anxiety.

In past dating experiences, I relied heavily on the liquid courage alcohol provided. I loved how it loosened me up and helped me present myself a certain way—discriminating, intellectual, and cultured. Without it, I had to experience the full awkwardness and uncertainty of the situation.

I went out on many first dates. The pocket square-toting American of English heritage who was obsessed with being Italian; the former Olympic bobsledder who resembled a young Christopher Reeve and who walked out on me when he realized I favored gun regulation; the businessman who resembled a crazed Jack Nicholson when he laughed. Most of the men I met were nice; a few were mean. Some dates were enjoyable experiences even if they didn't lead to anything. Others provided cringe-worthy tales to share with my girlfriends. And some just left me feeling confused and wondering whether I was ready.

All of these first dates had one thing in common: the issue of my not drinking arose within the first ten minutes. Apparently, few of them had paid attention to the part of my profile where I made this clear, or they just didn't believe me. After saying "I don't drink anymore," their faces would freeze, like they were waiting for the punch line: "I don't drink any less, either." Others responded warily, "Why is that?" or "Was it a problem for you?"

At first I took the honest route. I told them, "I decided it was better for me not to drink." But this inevitably led to more questions like "Is there a story there?" Or an awkward silence that cast a dark cloud over the remainder of the evening. I knew that an honest conversation about my drinking might occur at some point but didn't have to happen on the first date.

In an attempt to draw the focus away from my teetotaling and toward my sparkling sense of humor, I came up with a few responses to introduce some levity:

- "It's a condition of my parole"
- "It interacts with my, um, medication" [widened eyes for emphasis]
- "I took E/snorted a few lines earlier and I never mix"
- "It's bad for the baby"

Unfortunately, my snarky responses often had unintended effects. Though I meant to buy some time for us to get to know one another without undue focus on my not drinking, instead I created a barrier of sorts, a divide between myself and someone I might have gotten to know better had things been less complicated. And it was difficult to forge any real connection without that level of honesty. Besides, they usually didn't leave it alone; even after responding in a way that should have communicated that I didn't want to discuss it, many of them pressed me for an explanation. I got the message that my not drinking was a real issue for these guys. Whether they were uncomfortable drinking alone or had preconceived notions about people who chose not to drink alcohol, I'm not sure. But after one of these interactions, I typically didn't hear from them again.

I did meet one man who seemed nice enough and who was unfazed by my newfound sobriety; he could take or leave alcohol. But he was wrong for me in just about every other way: newly divorced and jaded, with a young son, and an unwillingness to go outside of his fairly limited comfort zone (and zip code). For two months I tolerated this utterly forgettable man, who told me our relationship "was fine for now, but I'm just taking it weekend to weekend" before I realized I could do better. A lot better. I closed my Match.com account and decided to focus on my friends for a while.

Chapter 14

Drinking Buddies

One of my biggest fears about quitting drinking was how it would change friendships. Alcohol seemed to be a bond I shared with many friends and without it, I feared we would part ways. But after I quit drinking, I was surprised by what actually happened. Some friendships were seamless, and some fizzled, while others grew stronger.

I met Lila and Grace (names have been changed to protect the mostly innocent) when I started working for a continuing medical education company in Boston. Lila interviewed me for the position; we bonded over our love of dogs and how to manage foot pain from running. Grace and I started working at the company on the same day. Soon we began to spend time together outside of work. After hours, we could frequently be found at Cuff's, the bar in the police-station-cum-hotel down the street from the office. The long hours we put in at the office were occasionally rewarded with an open bar on the company tab. This time spent together, talking shop with drinks in hand, strengthened our relationships as colleagues and friends and forged a camaraderie we needed when traveling around the country to present medical conferences. On the road, we endured endless conference days and extended expense-account dinners, which always included cocktails and fine wines.

It was toward the end of my job with Lila and Grace that I finally stopped drinking. They had watched me quit before only to start again. And I had subjected them to my thoughtful contemplations about drinking while we threw back juicy chardonnays. Both came from families where alcoholism was present. Lila's father was an active alcoholic who quit and relapsed countless times, while both of Grace's parents had suffered with alcoholism; her mother quit cold turkey years earlier while her father went the classic AA route and had two decades of sobriety.

Lila and Grace were supportive of my quitting drinking and deferred to me when we went out to dinner, asking whether I minded if they had wine while I abstained. It was then that I realized the different relationships Lila and Grace had with alcohol. Lila enjoyed drinking but she didn't drink every day; she overdid it occasionally but alcohol didn't have the same grip on her that it did on me. To our friendship, my quitting drinking wasn't even a speed bump.

Grace's relationship with alcohol was more complicated. The fact that I spoke so openly about my concerns before quitting and my experience since allowed her to open up about her own alcohol issues. She shared her experience growing up in a chaotic, alcoholic environment; how before her father got sober, the family never knew whether to expect the peaceful patriarch or a raving lunatic. She confided that she often wondered if it wouldn't be better for her to quit drinking too. A few times she told me she was just coming out of a particularly difficult time, that she had been drinking a lot at home alone, using alcohol to ease her suffering. But that she was now not drinking. She spoke so candidly at these times and was so earnest in her desire to do the right thing for herself; my response was like those of my friends a few years before: I congratulated her for being so honest with herself. But after such a conversation, there was often a period of silence between us. I deduced that it was during these silences, or when we were together but she didn't raise the issue of her drinking, that she had resumed. That no news was not good news.

Simon was someone I would have called a drinking buddy. He and I went out to gay bars and straight bars and drank cocktail after cocktail. Eyes narrowed, voices raised, and speech slurred, we would flirt with the people around us and vehemently argue whatever ridiculous point we thought we were making. Stumbling home, we were often too out of it to be really concerned about our own or one another's safety.

After I stopped drinking, however, my friendship with Simon evolved. While we still occasionally went to bars together—he would order his usual Cape Codder while I sipped seltzer with lime—we did other things too. We went to horror movies or chick flicks, walked around Cambridge and Boston, and met for coffee or Indian buffet. During those times, I had an opportunity to get to know Simon in a different way than when we were drinking together. I learned about his extensive knowledge of, eclectic taste in, and extremely strong opinions about music; heard stories about what it was like to grow up gay in rural upstate New York; and found out what he really thought about my ex-boyfriends. Most of all, I had the privilege to discover Simon as he was, with all his beautiful quirks, wisdom, and humor.

One friendship ended unexpectedly. Ned was about my dad's age. We met when he lived in the apartment upstairs from me in Boston's North End and we became one another's confidant. Ned and I didn't drink together, save for the occasional glass of wine (one for him, two for me) at his favorite pizza place. We preferred long walks to Harvard Square, six miles during which he told me his stories and I told him mine. Despite our nearly 30-year age difference, Ned and I were at similar stages of self-discovery, especially when it came to relationships, and we often discussed our love interests, or lack thereof. Our exchanges were quid pro quo, very balanced unless one of us was experiencing a particular relationship crisis.

After I quit drinking and everything in my life seemed to go wrong, Ned was in a stable relationship and needed our friendship less. My need to talk through difficult emotions increased, perhaps too much for him, and when we spoke I sensed his impatience. At times we could only connect for a brief phone call that I had to schedule with him days in advance.

I realized that my friendship with Ned no longer provided what it once had; that what began as mutual respect and friendship had devolved into rote exchanges in which Ned assigned himself a superior role. I told him how I felt, that I was glad he had found happiness in a relationship and that our ten-year friendship meant a lot to me, but that it could not continue in its current state. That was the last time we communicated.

Because drinking was often present when I spent time with friends, my perception of those friendships also tended to be under the influence. Once I stopped, I realized that some of the people I thought were drinking buddies were true friends, while other friendships might have lasted beyond their natural expiration dates. It wasn't until I removed the filter of alcohol that I could see this clearly.

Chapter 15

Dancing on my Own

Apart from Simon, I didn't go out with friends very much, especially at night. It was too difficult to imagine being in the same places and not ordering a cocktail. I had so many anxieties: *Would I have fun? Would everyone think I'm boring? Would they be boring? Would I mistakenly be served a drink containing alcohol? Would I lose my willpower and order a martini? Would everyone notice my not drinking? Would no one notice? What the hell am I going to drink?*

Any time I did go to a bar, it felt as if I was the only one not drinking. And it seemed that everyone with a cocktail, beer, or glass of wine in his or her hand was having a great time, a much better time than me. Squeezing between patrons and leaning into the bar to order a club soda with lime just didn't pack the same punch as ordering a Jamesons on the rocks. And a couple of times I spied bartenders glancing at my stomach to see if I was pregnant, perhaps the only socially acceptable reason to abstain. Standing there among people yelling and straining to hear, or looking over my shoulder to see if there was someone more interesting to talk to, got old quickly. Just as my friends were warming up, I was ready to go home.

One night I went to a concert with Simon at the House of Blues. As soon as we arrived, it was clear that it was not my scene. The singer was a Swedish pop star who attracted a very cool crowd, mostly handsome young gay men wearing tight T-shirts and carrying bright red Solo cups. I was one of the oldest and most conservatively dressed and again felt like the only one not drinking. At first, I was also the only one not dancing. Previously alcohol made dancing possible because it diminished my self-consciousness. Now, without a drink in hand, moving my body seemed out of the question. But then something unexpected happened: a song struck me as particularly dance-worthy and my shoulders and hips began to move with the beat. I must have looked like the Tin Man, newly oiled and jerking about. But I didn't care. I was completely sober and dancing. And for a few moments I didn't feel so alone in the crowd.

Going out to dinner was easier than going to bars and clubs. I learned that the hardest part was the first 15 minutes, when people perused the wine list, procured tastes, swirled, sniffed, and sipped. Inevitably the aroma of someone's wine would drift into my nostrils making my envious head spin. After 15 minutes, though, people settled into their meals and their conversations and my anxiety abated.

One night, I went out with a good friend and two of her friends to celebrate one of their birthdays. As I primped for the evening, my brain was addled by familiar anxieties: *Would they like me? Would I say something stupid? Would I feel left out? Would they remember I'd only had sparkling water when it comes time to split the check?*

At the restaurant, my awareness of alcohol was as heightened as ever. The three bottles of wine ordered by the table to our left to loosen up an awkward double date, the shots delivered to the table of rowdy 22-year-olds to our right, the three rounds enjoyed by my friends, while I sipped greedily at my Perrier. When we finished dinner and paid the check (which they graciously adjusted for me), they discussed where to go next. But my destination was already decided. Going to a bar at midnight after a lovely dinner used to be my favorite way to spend a Saturday evening. But it was simply lost on me that night. I hugged my friend, wished the group a good night, and jumped in a cab.

Chapter 16

Are You There God? It's Me, Jenna

As often happens during life's transitions and trying times, I began to think more about spirituality. This was hardly the first time the subject had occurred to me. From an early age, I was concerned with religion and spirituality. As for every other American girl growing up in the 1980s, Judy Blume's *Are You There God? It's Me, Margaret* was required reading. This quintessential coming of age story focused on the sixth-grade Margaret, as she dealt with boobs, bras, boys, and first periods. Because Margaret's Christian mom and Jewish dad chose not to bring her up in a particular faith—instead offering her the option of finding her own way—Margaret became obsessed with her relationship with God, exploring the faith and religious beliefs of those around her and having a series of conversations with Him that began, *Are you there God? It's me, Margaret…*

I was raised Catholic and, like Margaret, I took my relationship with God very seriously. I prayed every night on a blue crystal and silver rosary given to me by my mother's mother, pausing on each bead and silently mouthing the words. She told me it contained a drop of holy water that was blessed by the Pope, and I kept the beloved beads under my pillow. I attended Sunday services regularly and with piety. After listening to a particular homily, I took care not to just ask God for things in my prayers, but to offer thanks for what I already had, to express gratitude for the health of my family, and

51

to care for those less fortunate. I was christened, communion-ed, and confirmed.

I loved how the church had an explanation for everything. To a confused and fearful ten-year-old, that kind of certainty was the answer to my prayers. Gradually, though, I had more and more questions about the church. So many things didn't add up. Among the most troubling concepts was that of original sin. I wondered how every person, from the moment of his or her birth, could already be guilty of some grave wrongdoing. The church taught me that I was born bad and would spend my life hoping to be saved.

As I grew older and more aware, my misgivings with the church extended beyond the basic dogma. Other doctrine grated on me and smacked more of a desire to control than to inspire. Masturbation—bad. Sex before marriage—bad. Contraception—bad. Homosexuality—bad. For a bunch of old men who (allegedly) never had sex, they sure had a lot of opinions about it. I realized that even though the church claimed to have all the answers, they probably weren't the right ones for me. In my late teenage years, my relationship with the Catholic Church was on again off again. By my early twenties I stopped attending services, stopped praying to God, and started wandering about without any spiritual path. I felt that I couldn't practice the faith in which I was raised and everything else seemed like someone else's religion.

When I felt plagued by uncertainty and confusion, I missed having a framework that would help me to look at my situation and wished for a set of beliefs that would provide some perspective. Feeling lost had made it easy to reach for the anesthesia of alcohol; without it, I felt the spiritual void even more acutely.

Chapter 17

You Have to Run Before You Can Sit

Without a specific set of spiritual beliefs, I relied more heavily on my physical experience of life. I decided to try running. Again. I ran in high school but never well. On the track team, there were two options: long, slow distance or short, fast sprints. I had neither the lithe physique that lends itself to mile after mile nor the thick muscular set that could set records for the 100-yard dash. The category in which I would have excelled—slow, short distance—did not exist.

I was, however, a born power walker. With long legs and a New York sense of urgency, walking fast came naturally. It was my exercise of choice and preferred mode of transportation. I logged many miles walking around what I came to think of as the Charles River treadmill, a four-mile loop that went from the Boston Esplanade, to the Museum of Science, across the docks of Cambridge, and over the Mass Ave Bridge. The wind in my hair, the chop of the water, and the energy of the other people—I found walking exhilarating. But something was missing.

Since my high school track days, I tried running several times but it never took. I usually started off too fast and burned out before I'd gotten far, which was both painful and discouraging. My memory of running was one of discomfort and inadequacy. I couldn't run fast or far so I wondered *why bother?* Yet, as runners passed me on my daily walks, I yearned to follow them, to break free of what had become a predictable stride, even if it meant falling, failing, or just looking stupid.

When I decided to give running another chance, it was the middle of July and Boston was sweltering (in retrospect, starting to run at that time of year might have been analogous to quitting drinking during the December holidays, intensity-wise). Leaving my apartment and running toward the Charles River treadmill, I couldn't make it more than a half-mile. I dripped with sweat and wheezed asthmatically. My legs felt like they might go out from under me. I had to stop and walk.

With my hands on my hips and my head cast downward, I already felt defeated. My first instinct was to turn around and go home. After all, I had not made it very far. But I stayed with that thought as I placed one foot in front of the other. After a few minutes of walking, I felt my heart rate slowing down and my legs regaining strength. I listened to my body with each step and each breath and noticed the small changes that occurred. I recognized that I had come up against an edge, my edge at that moment, but that perhaps it wasn't a fixed edge. I needed to slow down but perhaps I could start again in a little while. After a few more minutes of walking, I started to run again, a little slower this time, and tried to reach the next milestone.

This went on for months: run, walk, run, walk, run, walk. With practice I could run to more distant milestones before needing to stop and walk. The community boathouse. Then the softball fields. Then the Museum of Science. Progress was not linear but I could feel myself getting stronger. Some days I got cocky and ran so fast I had to stop after just a few minutes. Other days my body felt wooden and heavy, and I walked more than I ran. Occasionally running felt effortless and poignant, like I was on the brink of a breakthrough. Each experience was different in some way; no two runs were alike.

What made this attempt at running different from previous ones? I seemed to focus more on the experience of running rather than on the outcome, my speed or distance. I paid attention to what physical sensations and emotions arose from moment to moment, before, during, and after a run. I saw how slowing down allowed me to go further, continuously, and to gradually work up to a faster pace and longer distance. By focusing inward, I began to experience each step, and each breath, and to practice staying in the present moment.

I began to see a parallel between running and not drinking: rather than avoiding discomfort, I was developing curiosity about it. I was looking at the quality of my experience rather than simply labeling it good (and grasping to keep it) or bad (and scrambling to dodge it). With running, I chose to do something that felt new and uncomfortable because it was challenging and rewarding. Running required patience. It required that I be gentle with myself, and that I listen to my body. These were qualities I found difficult to practice in other parts of my life.

Chapter 18

Amore Senza Vino

Having dipped my toe into the discomfort pool with running, I decided to do something really dangerous. I started seeing a man I had dated years earlier, the same Sicilian scientist who missed my book party the night I got wasted and left my laptop computer in a cab. After we broke up a few years earlier, he moved to New York City to start his own lab. We reconnected via Facebook and met for dinner one night when I was in town helping Lila look for an apartment. Sitting across from him at an elegant Japanese restaurant, I felt that old spark. We reminisced about our first date, when we met in a Boston coffee shop and I suggested he get *The Elements of Style* to help him write his first big scientific paper (he went to the bookstore that afternoon to buy it). We told one another what had happened in our lives since we had last talked. We discussed our families, our jobs, and how much had changed. I told him I had quit drinking, and he was impressed. He still made goofy jokes that would only be funny to a native Italian speaker who now spoke mostly in English; the jokes themselves were terrible but his utter delight with them made me laugh despite my best efforts. After dinner, he showed me the building where he worked, the lab he built. Humble to a fault, he came as close to bragging as I had ever seen him. I knew he was not just proud of his accomplishments, but excited to share them with me.

For a few months after that night we stayed in touch but didn't see one another. I was still cautious about dating and he didn't push too hard. It wasn't until he pulled a little April Fool's Day joke and changed his relationship status on Facebook to "married" that I nearly jumped out of my chair and realized how strongly I still felt for him. A month later, we were in Washington DC for different professional conferences and thus began our long-distance romance. It comprised long weekends in New York and Boston, phone calls and Skype sessions, and a lot of texting. Soon I was falling in love sober for the first time since high school. But without the buffer of alcohol, I felt unprotected from all of the awkward, insecure, and anxious moments of new-old love. At times the fear of loving someone who had hurt and disappointed me was overwhelming, and I wasn't sure if I was capable of the forgiveness and trust that was necessary to move forward. All at once it seemed I was on the brink of something potentially great and extremely perilous, like walking a high wire without a net. I needed guidance.

Much like I contemplated changing my drinking habits for years before ever taking action, I had long considered meditating. I read about it extensively, but never actually sat down to do it. Meditation was something I idealized; it was part of the person I wanted to become. And I wondered whether it was the missing link that would help me face my fears, anxiety, and self-doubt—the things I drank to avoid.

I went to my bookshelf and pulled out *The Wisdom of a Broken Heart*, Susan Piver's guide to dealing with heartbreak that involves seeing it as potentially transformative. Though I didn't have a broken heart per se, I identified with her description of heartbreak's rawness and vulnerability, which I had felt since I quit drinking and especially since I embarked on a new relationship. In that relationship—and in life—I wanted to feel the full range of emotions without either giving up too much of myself or completely shutting down.

Susan's book also provided meditation instruction. As I was reading one night, with some trepidation, I slid from my bed to the floor, two pillows strategically arranged beneath me. I set a timer for ten minutes and tried to follow those instructions:

Body: sit in a comfortable, uplifted, cross-legged position with a straight, unsupported back, the hands palms down on the thighs, and the eyes open to gaze softly at a spot about six feet away on the floor.

Breath: place awareness on the breath coming in and going out through the nose.

Mind: rather than trying not to think, place awareness on the breath; when thoughts inevitably draw the attention away, label them "thinking" and gently return attention to the breath.

My first meditation session went roughly like this:

> *OK, my attention is on the breath. IN, OUT, IN, OUT, IN, OUT. I never noticed how some of the whorls on the chest of drawers in front of me look like a big brown bear peeking out from behind a tree. My boyfriend leaves for Sicily shortly, I wonder if I'll hear from him. I hate my hips; they're so tight. I can't even sit correctly for meditation. Maybe I'll take the long way to work tomorrow so I can pick up an iced coffee. Wait, I'm supposed to be focusing on the breath. IN, OUT, IN. Can you imagine if I tried to do this at my parents' house, with the telephone ringing off the hook and people knocking down my door? I should text my boyfriend and say, "have a good trip" or should I say, "have a good flight?" Oh, shit. IN, OUT, IN, OUT. How many minutes do I have left? I'm not sure I can do this every day. Maybe I should set an alarm on my phone to remind me to meditate every day. What am I going to do with the cats so they don't distract me? IN, OUT. How long do I have to do this before I feel better? I have to pee.*

That was the first 30 seconds.

The next day I reached out to Susan directly. We had met years before but had not kept in touch. I told her I had tried to meditate and she graciously offered to introduce me to the practice she described in her book. A few days later, I visited her at her home and she asked me why now felt like the right time to start meditating. Almost as soon as I opened my mouth, I was sobbing. I told Susan about my decision to stop drinking, how I had used alcohol to deal with difficult emotions and to fill in the empty spaces of my life. I told her I was falling in love with someone who hurt me years earlier and that it was the first time since I'd stopped drinking that I felt so strongly for someone. I told her how precarious and hopeful I felt.

"It's not surprising that you feel this way," she said, "You've opened your heart to someone and that's good. You want to learn how to remain open and have stability." This was exactly how I felt. I knew I didn't want to close my heart; that was no way to live and certainly no way to love. I just didn't want to feel like my heart might explode at any moment.

We moved into to Susan's office. She lit two oil lamps and we sat on cushions facing her meditation shrine. She explained that the practice she described in her book is called Shamatha, which means peacefully abiding. In a quiet, steady voice, Susan provided meditation instruction on the body, breath, and mind. She didn't instruct me to not think or to go to my happy place. She spoke of developing curiosity about the mind, of how the body is both strong and soft, and how attention to the breath is both gentle and precise.

My eyes fell lightly on a spot along the border of the silk cloth lining the shrine and I sent out my breath and drew it back like waves gently rushing the shore and receding. In the ten minutes we practiced together, I didn't think about whether I should be somewhere else. I didn't think of work or to-do lists or even my fears about my new love. I'm sure that some thoughts came and went, but my overall experience was one of calm, something I hadn't felt in some time. I was hooked.

Before I left that day, Susan's one piece of advice regarding meditation practice was just to relax—not to zone out or will my mind to be blank, but to be however I am, whether that meant sad or anxious or happy or boring. The next day I sat alone on my bedroom floor, pillows sticking out from every which way to support my tight hips. I programmed my newly downloaded iPhone meditation app for ten minutes and started to meditate.

Chapter 19

Sit. Stay.

Alone in my own apartment, meditating didn't feel nearly as calm and comfortable as it did with Susan. Instead of the peaceful ebb and flow of waves lapping the shore, my awareness of the breath felt like the choppy waters of a rip tide. If I programmed my meditation timer for ten minutes, it took nearly all of that time to just find a comfortable position. Though the instructions were simple enough, nothing felt more difficult.

While I was practicing, I noticed how frequently my mind was off somewhere else, separate from my physical body and disconnected from the present moment. It was like fly paper, seeking out something to stick to. Once it found an interesting thought, it would turn it over and over, ruminating, judging, and creating a narrative. Many of these thoughts were about the ordinary administrivia of day-to-day life. Like little flies buzzing overhead, I thought, *What am I going to eat for breakfast?* or *I need to pick up stamps.* Other times the thoughts felt more troubling. Situations and people from my past—how I had been hurt or disappointed, how I had hurt or disappointed others, regrets. And my fledgling relationship provided particularly fertile ground for fantasizing about the future. While some days I imagined us picking out artwork for our new apartment, other days I imagined our breakup and feared growing old alone. Obsessing over the past or fantasizing about the future could easily spin out of control on the meditation cushion, to the point of completely losing awareness of the breath.

Remembering the instruction, though, whether the thoughts were mundane, profound, or painful, I tried first to notice them, then to label them "thinking," and finally to return my awareness to my current surroundings, my body sitting on the cushion, my breath coming in and going back out. By doing this, I began to view my thoughts differently. I realized I had a sort of allegiance to the drama of discursiveness, its distracting entertainment, the comfort, predictability, and certainty it provided. I could easily nestle into that discursiveness like I used to nestle into my favorite chair with a glass of wine.

By looking at my mind in this way, I realized I could choose where to place my attention. And this realization followed me into my life off the cushion. Whenever I experienced uncomfortable, uncertain, or painful thoughts and emotions, I found myself tolerating them a little more, not automatically reacting to them or avoiding them. When I became scared or insecure in my long-distance relationship, I noticed the desire to run away, not to feel the discomfort, or my wish for certainty and reassurance that everything would be OK.

By noticing these subtle changes, I felt encouraged to continue practicing meditation and to have faith in the process. When sitting felt impossible and I wanted to get up off my cushion and distract myself with TV, a snack, or some other form of entertainment, I tried to keep my seat. When it felt like a waste of time, when I was only aware of the breath for one minute out of ten, or when I felt emotions even more strongly and painfully than before, I tried to keep my seat. Something told me that sitting still with myself was the only key to a door I needed to open. And recognizing that a large part of the practice was just resisting the urge to give up—even if I was having the worst practice of my life—allowed me to stay.

Chapter 20

Mind the Gap

As I continued to practice meditation, I became more familiar with my mind, my habitual thoughts, my patterns of reactivity, and the stories I created about myself. I observed my preference for certainty and my wish to know what to expect in the future. Not knowing often led me to imagine the worst-case scenario (WCS), reasoning that if I could imagine the WCS and prepare myself for it, then I would (A) feel less pain/anxiety/upheaval when it happened or (B) be pleasantly surprised when it did not. Even though I did this enough times to know I never accurately predicted the WCS—and in the process I made my present much less pleasant—that did not stop me from trying.

While meditating one morning, I began to go down the WCS rabbit hole. I was considering moving to New York to be closer to my boyfriend but then found myself imagining all the negative outcomes: *We might break up, then I would be single on an island already full of single women, most of them younger and prettier than me, I can't compete with those women, I would need to lose 20 pounds and buy a whole new wardrobe, I might not be able to afford living there by myself, what if I had to move back in with my parents, what if I lost my job, what if my nieces who live in Massachusetts forget who I am...*

And then something shifted and I noticed a small space opening up between those rapid-fire thoughts. I realized that none of those things had happened or would necessarily happen. That if something did go wrong in my relationship, I could deal with it then. And I saw that I could turn my attention back toward the current moment—that it was where my real life was unfolding—rather than solidifying habitual thought patterns born of seeking impossible predictability and non-existent safety.

Off the cushion I also experienced such gaps. One night, about a month before I moved from Boston to New York, I was walking home from Cambridge after having dinner with Simon. The weather was pleasant, not too hot or too cold. A temperate breeze blew and there was a sort of electricity in the air. Walking across the Longfellow Bridge, I stopped to look at the Charles River, glittering with the lights of Back Bay, while the T rumbled into Charles Street station behind me. Standing there, I felt a sense of magic, something almost sacred.

What made this experience stand out from the millions of other moments I experienced every day? For a few moments I was fully present, mind and body synchronized as in meditation. Previously I might have thrown away such a moment, when I was going from point A to point B and the space in between was just a means to an end. But that night, though I hadn't yet reached my destination, I felt I had arrived. Some space arose between thoughts about packing boxes, planning every aspect of my move, and imagining all the things that might go wrong. And for a while, I hung out in that space.

Chapter 21

Falling off the (Dharma) Wagon

E ven though meditation had clear benefits, at times I just couldn't get to the cushion. Sometimes I was too busy, once in a while I forgot, but usually when I stopped meditating it was because I was feeling particularly anxious or depressed. Ironic, perhaps, since that was when I could have used the support of meditation the most—when it would have been helpful to remember that on the meditation cushion, and in life, all emotional states are welcome. The strong negative emotions that caused me to stop meditating were compounded by guilt about not meditating, which continued to keep me from the cushion.

As with any other meditation-related question, this led me back to Susan. I told her I had stopped meditating and wanted to begin again but that huge (albeit imaginary) boundaries made this seem impossible. And as always, her advice was, "Be gentle with yourself; don't be so hard on yourself." She suggested I sit for just five minutes, as a means of re-entry, and then to resume my regular practice the following day. But above all she emphasized that I should not berate myself for not meditating; that would defeat the purpose of this gentle, loving practice. Susan's other advice was to start reading the dharma—Buddhist teachings, sometimes referred to simply as "the truth."

I remembered a book by the American Buddhist nun Pema Chodron that I had purchased years earlier; I had started to read it but stopped because I wasn't ready to try the meditation practices she wrote about. Now that I was practicing meditation regularly (except for when I wasn't), I had a basis from which to understand the teachings.

At home I went back to my bookshelf and pulled down *The Places that Scare You*. I sprawled out on my bed and began to read. Within moments I was nodding and underlining passages, feeling as though I could have written some of them myself. It was as if I knew these things but had just forgotten. Early in the book, she writes about training in bodhichitta, the awakened heart or soft spot we all possess that allows us to love and feel compassion:

> *"Wherever we are, we can train as a warrior. The practices of meditation, loving-kindness, compassion, joy, and equanimity are our tools. With the help of these practices, we can uncover the soft spot of bodhichitta. We will find it behind the hardness of rage and in the shakiness of fear. It is available in loveliness as well as in kindness.*

> *Many of us prefer practices that will not cause discomfort, yet at the same time we want to be healed. But bodhichitta training doesn't work that way. A warrior accepts that we can never know what will happen to us next. We can try to control the uncontrollable by looking for security and predictability, always hoping to be comfortable and safe. But the truth is that we can never avoid uncertainty. This not knowing is part of the adventure, and it's also what makes us afraid.*

> *Bodhichitta training offers no promise of happy endings. Rather, this 'I' who wants to find security—who wants something to hold on to—can finally learn to grow up. The central question of a warrior's training is not how we avoid uncertainty and fear but how we relate to discomfort. How do we practice with difficulty, with our emotions, with the unpredictable encounters of an ordinary day?"*

In this tradition, a warrior was not someone who was violent or aggressive; rather she was someone who was willing to deal with the nature of reality and to greet it with softness and love. As confusing and chaotic and sad as the world could seem at times, the warrior maintained an open heart, and continued to open rather than to shut down. And the basis for that gentleness, that ability to open, was meditation.

I knew these things to be true but previously was not ready to hear them: I knew that avoiding discomfort would never allow me to live life fully. I knew that my desire to eradicate uncertainty and fear would never be satisfied. In a way, I even knew that the sadness and vulnerability that lurked beneath my accumulated distractions was also a strength, an indication of my capacity for love.

Chapter 22

Practicing Imperfection

I read every Pema Chodron book I could get my hands on, from *Start Where You Are* to *Comfortable with Uncertainty* to *Taking the Leap*. I found the notion of starting where you are particularly poignant. Since I was a girl, I never felt that I was enough. As a result, I became preoccupied with self-improvement. "You can never be too rich, too beautiful, or too thin" grew to include "too intelligent, too well liked, or too accomplished." I developed the capacity to continually critique myself and always to find ways in which to improve. At some point off in the future, when I had reached perfection, I believed my real life would begin.

Reading the dharma allowed me to consider the possibility that I already had everything I needed. That I was already enough. I realized that not feeling lovable and acceptable was the cause of the discomfort I had long tried to cover up, that my drinking was a tactic I used to mitigate the pain I caused myself by trying to be perfect. Just as I delved into the subtle questions about my alcohol use, I now found myself asking questions about my addiction to self-improvement. Where did it come from? How did it manifest? What might it be costing me?

By contemplating these questions, I saw how deep the roots of my striving for perfection had grown. That it seemed to touch nearly everything I believed or did. I remembered the time I pretended I was asleep when my painfully shy high school sweetheart finally kissed me because I couldn't take responsibility for my own raging teenage hormones. I recalled the countless classes in which I obsessed over how to ask the most brilliant and astounding question in order to gain the admiration of the teacher and my fellow students (thereby missing the dialog that would have made my question even remotely relevant). I tried to tabulate the vast amounts of money (and time) I spent on cosmetics, skin care products, and laser procedures to improve the appearance of my skin. I saw myself showering, getting dressed, and applying those expensive cosmetics with the lights out because I couldn't bear to see my imperfect face and body in the mirror. I realized how I compared myself with every woman I met since the age of about ten on a complex scale involving measures of age, beauty, fitness, intelligence, interestingness, sexiness, and desirability. I recalled countless instances in which I bottled up my feelings (and later exploded) because I was afraid of losing someone's love. I saw myself perseverating on small tasks like cleaning and organizing because they gave me the illusion of control. I saw myself failing to give my full attention to any number of work or writing projects because I feared that I would not do them perfectly.

I remembered how I spent countless hours tipsy at home alone after work because I felt paralyzed, unsure of how to move my life in the right direction. I imagined all the opportunities I missed during that time because I wasn't guaranteed of their perfect outcome. I saw myself using alcohol to make good experiences feel even better and to obliterate negative ones because perfection demanded that I always be smiling, happy, upbeat, and having a great time.

In examining my allegiance to self-improvement, I was astounded by the breadth and depth of the perfection propaganda I had absorbed. How I had sculpted my expectations, thoughts, and behaviors based on the messages I received from my childhood, parents, family, friends, television, advertising, movies, magazines, marketing, dating, and work. Almost without noticing, I had absorbed and accepted as truth all of the ways in which I wasn't enough. And this determined how I viewed myself and the world. As a result, I lost sight of who I was at the core. I couldn't see the lovable, imperfect being who was there.

I began to wonder what would happen if (as pointed out to me by the same wise therapist who challenged me to try out life without alcohol) the consequences of just being my perfectly imperfect self were not so dire? What if there was nothing to fix?

One morning as I sat meditating, I heard myself silently intone, *In this moment, nothing is wrong.* For someone who habitually sought out problems to fix, imagined the worst-case scenario, and practiced emotional disaster preparedness, this thought was transformative. Practicing meditation had allowed me to cultivate enough space to let in a glimmer of a new thought: maybe things were just as they should be. Maybe I was just as I should be.

I came back to this idea many times both on and off the cushion: behind my discursiveness and habitual thoughts, there was actually nothing wrong. Weeks later, I recalled this notion while meditating again. Silently, I repeated to myself, *In this moment, there is nothing wrong.* I intended to label the thought "thinking" and to return to the breath. But instead, I heard another voice silently answer, *In this moment, there is nothing right, either.*

I remembered a quote from Hamlet that took on new significance: "For there is nothing either good or bad, but thinking makes it so." I realized that all of my judgments of things as good and bad, right and wrong, perfect or imperfect, all of the stories about why I wasn't enough—those were just thoughts. They weren't as real and solid as they seemed. If I paid attention to them, they would change—their nature, texture, and significance would shift ever so slightly from one moment to the next. My thoughts were not me. They were like passing clouds while I was like the blue sky, constant and unwavering.

Chapter 23

Resistance Is Futile

Studying the dharma brought me to the lojong or mind-training slogans of Atisha, a set of 59 Buddhist sayings that provide a framework for everyday thoughts and events, both on and off the cushion. Each contains lessons and meanings that could be probed for a lifetime. The first slogan, for example, "First, train in the preliminaries," refers to the four reminders: (1) the preciousness of human life and our good fortune to be able to hear the dharma, (2) the reality of death, that it will come suddenly and without warning, (3) the cause and effect nature of karma, and (4) the inevitability of suffering. The final slogan, "Don't expect applause," suggests that we should not expect others to notice when we practice or do good. I couldn't help but laugh at myself when I read this slogan since, when I first began meditating, I hoped for at least a golf clap. But after some time, I realized that this daily practice, much like brushing my teeth, was both mundane and essential for my wellbeing.

Some of the lojong slogans held particular significance for me, especially the eighth: "Three objects, three poisons, three seeds of virtue." The three objects are things we want, things we don't want, and things we ignore; the three poisons are passion, aggression, and ignorance; and the three seeds of virtue are freedom from passion, freedom from aggression, and freedom from ignorance. In delving deeper into this slogan, reading about it and contemplating it, I recognized how my drinking covered all of these bases. How I used drinking to hold on to pleasurable experiences way past their expiration date, how I never wanted the party to end and thought it couldn't end as long as I kept drinking. Other times I used alcohol to try to change the way things were, to aggressively counteract feelings of anxiety and fear, to replace them with the good times I thought were to be found in the bottle. Last, my drinking allowed me to zone out, to disconnect from issues that needed attention—a relationship that was hurtful, an unsatisfying career.

Alcohol was not inherently poisonous, but the way I used it was problematic. And while all three poisons were present at various times, one in particular predominated. In drinking and in life, I tended toward aggression, or as I thought of it, resistance. In my misguided pursuit of perfection, from the moment I woke up in the morning to the moment I fell asleep, my mind was in a constant state of resistance. *I should have done this...or that, I shouldn't feel this way, I wish I were more..., If only....* These were a constant refrain, like elevator Muzak that was playing in the background so long that I stopped noticing.

In *Start Where You Are*, Pema Chodron writes "resistance to unwanted circumstances has the power to keep those circumstances alive and well for a very long time." She also writes about how the three poisons can provide fertile ground for change, a rich source from which to pull self-awareness and gentleness, and to open up to the much wider possibilities life has to offer. But in order to do this, the first step is to accept things the way they are, to stop trying so hard to change them or even wish they were different. The most important lesson for me, I realized, was to see what was there, the nature of reality, to accept that, to love it, and to practice imperfection.

When I felt most confused, frustrated, and restless, when my issues felt stickier and ickier than I imagined others' to be, rather than wishing to vanquish those feelings, rather than making myself a strong cocktail to numb the discomfort, I could lean into them. Welcome them. In *The Wisdom of No Escape*, she writes:

> *"Sometimes the teachings emphasize the wisdom, brilliance, or sanity that we possess, and sometimes they emphasize the*

obstacles, how it is that we feel stuck in a small, dark place. These are actually two sides of one coin: when they are put together, inspiration (or well-being) and burden (or suffering) describe the human condition…we see how beautiful and wonderful and amazing things are, and we see how caught up we are. It isn't that one is the bad part and one is the good part, but that it's a kind of interesting, smelly, rich, fertile mess of stuff. When it's all mixed up together, it's us: humanness…even though there are so many teachings, so many meditations, so many instructions, the basic point of it all is just to learn to be extremely honest and also wholehearted about what exists in your mind…the whole thing that adds up to what we call 'me' or 'I.' Nobody else can really begin to sort out for you what to accept and what to reject in terms of what wakes you up and what makes you fall asleep."

My tendency toward aggression made me resist the confusion I often felt; I had a strong drive to exorcise it, and that was always easy with a drink (or three). But by resisting, I solidified my story, used it to go to sleep, rather than to wake up. If, on the other hand, I thought of what was going on in my life as what I had to work with, I realized that these were the very things that could help me wake up.

Chapter 24

Taking Refuge

Becoming a warrior. Touching the soft spot of bodhichitta. Cultivating compassion, joy, and equanimity. These aspects of the dharma made sense to me like a foreign language suddenly crossing over into fluency. Yet, one of the most basic concepts in Buddhism continued to elude me.

By contrast with original sin, the foundational Buddhist concept of basic goodness holds that humans are essentially good, clear-seeing, loving, and compassionate by nature. When I first learned about basic goodness, it was difficult to think of myself in this light. As a life-long self-doubter and self-improver, it was easier to see the basic goodness in others than in myself. Yet something about this concept spoke to me on a deep level.

After much practice, contemplation, and conversation with Susan, I decided to formalize my commitment to the Buddhist path. Doing so is called taking the refuge vow, in which one takes refuge in the three jewels: the Buddha, the dharma, and the sangha. We take refuge in the Buddha as an example of a human being who attained enlightenment. We take refuge in the dharma, the teachings of the Buddha on the nature of reality. And we take refuge in the sangha, the community of practitioners who are all on their own lonely paths but who are also there to support one another.

In taking the refuge vow, essentially I became a refugee. As Chogyam Trungpa put it, "The bad news is you're falling through the air, nothing to hang on to, no parachute. The good news is there's no ground." I committed to the practice of sitting with impermanence, uncertainty, discomfort, and imperfection, not to run away or try to reframe these things in more pleasant ways. I committed to dealing with life as it is, to accepting myself as I am, to being compassionate toward others, and to having a sense of humor.

As part of the ceremony I was given a Tibetan name—Champa Wangmo—which translates roughly to "maitri lady." Maitri has been described by many Buddhist teachers as an unconditional friendliness, toward others and especially toward oneself; Susan has described it as an antidote to self-doubt. To my understanding, maitri is not about aggressively countering doubt by beating my breast and proclaiming all my wonderful, lovable qualities. And not about managing or forgiving myself for being scared or petty or small-minded. My understanding about maitri (and I am sure that this will continue to evolve over the course of my lifetime) is that it's about opening to myself with the same sense of love and welcome that I have for others.

After taking refuge, my thoughts and emotions became Technicolor in nature. My fears and self-doubt were magnified, and I had an increasing sense of groundlessness. At first I reached out to friends and family to talk through my discomfort, to find some consolation, for someone to reassure me. But the feelings remained. After a few days of utter tumult and confusion, I realized that this was exactly what I signed up for. That every experience—every moment—was an opportunity to wake up, rather than to grasp or repel or go to sleep. And that what I was looking for was not *out there*, it was in me. Right where it always was. Each time I criticized, or doubted, or judged myself, I tried to rouse a sense of friendliness and love for this person struggling and feeling pain, for this person who was just fine. I realized that maitri or loving-kindness—turning toward all of the scary, uncomfortable feelings with softness and a sense of welcome—would become the practice of my lifetime. Applying the same warm welcome I would for anyone coming to my home, I thought, *How can I care for you? What can I do to show you my love? You are welcome here.*

78

Afterword

I Will Always Love Booze

We have kept alcohol in the house since I quit drinking. Wine, gin, beer, and Italian liqueurs. I have never had a drop. This is partially because I have trained myself not to see the booze or to view it the way someone with a severe peanut allergy would look at a Reese's Peanut Butter Cup. The other part is that I have willingly chosen—over and over and over again—not to drink.

One night a few months after taking the refuge vow, the Sicilian scientist brought home a bottle of ten-year-old single-malt scotch. Scotch never appealed to me, but for some reason this lone bottle had a different effect than all the other bottles that came and went without incident. The night he brought it home, he poured a meager amount into an ice-filled glass, and sipped at it leisurely. As with any time he drank, I was reminded of how different our relationships with alcohol are. Even though he grew up in a country where alcohol was not restricted until a certain age, he could take or leave it. When he did drink, he knew when he'd had enough and never hesitated to leave a half-glass of wine behind, whereas I would let the amount of wine left in the glass (and let's be honest, the bottle) dictate how much I drank. More was always better for me, while his approach to drinking was driven by internal cues.

When I caught a whiff of the scotch that night, it turned my stomach, and transported me. Its smoky-oakiness reminded me of my last night in Oaxaca about ten years earlier. A night I drank far too

79

much mezcal and ate nothing but the accompanying orange wedges and a handful of cayenne-fried crickets. On the overnight bus ride back to Mexico City, I threw up into a bag of souvenirs I'd purchased from Oaxacan artisans, surrounded by what I'd imagine were several native Mexicans rolling their eyes at the dumb drunk gringa. Like a lot of my darkest drinking moments, this happened while I was alone, or at least not surrounded by people I knew and who could hold me accountable. Perhaps this was part of what allowed me to think I didn't have a drinking problem for so many years.

A few days after my mental Mexican journey, my boyfriend did some actual traveling. He packed his carry-on and left for a business trip, obviously leaving the nearly full bottle of scotch sitting on our kitchen counter. Alone on the couch that night, I felt bored and lonely and desperate for a distraction. I ate an unsatisfying meal and watched back-to-back episodes of trashy TV. Still, an empty feeling persisted and I craved something to fill that void. I became very aware of the bottle of scotch in the next room. Even though the smell bordered on nauseating, I was acutely aware of the potential to be found there. Though I missed drinking a glass of wine at an event or having a cocktail with a friend, I really missed drinking alone. I missed the ritual and the predictable relief of it, like putting in foam earplugs that expanded to obliterate any unwanted noise. I missed nursing my feelings of loneliness, like wrapping myself in a warm blanket to ward off the cold. I missed the privacy of it, the indulgence of finishing a bottle of wine without the judgment of onlookers.

I remembered how satisfying alcohol was for me, at least in the short term. Without it, I often felt deprived. When I was drinking, an unsatisfying meal could be compensated for with an extra glass of wine. That same unsatisfying meal in the absence of alcohol felt much more troubling. There was a greater sense of urgency to fill that emptiness. Imported artichoke hearts, Marcona almonds, macadamia nuts, fine dark chocolate, and other indulgences became stand-ins for booze; I justified the expense with what I had given up.

A friend started drinking again after quitting for more than a year. Listening to her describe how she was able to drink moderately after a long pause made me envious. And fearful. Despite all the internal work I had done with meditation, I feared that nothing had changed in my relationship with alcohol except for my choice not to drink it.

If I were ever to pick up a glass of wine again it would have been on a business trip to Lyon, the gastronomic capital of France and therefore the world. I usually found that the first 15 minutes of a meal were the most uncomfortable for me, but in France all bets were off. The presence of wine and other alcohol in France was much more continuous, beginning with the assumption by flight attendants that a glass of wine would accompany whatever the airline placed on an eight-by-ten-inch plastic tray and called dinner. Continuing with the lengthy lunches that were much more likely to include wine than at home. And culminating in the sumptuous dinners, which began with an aperitif, proceeded with carefully selected wines, and finished with a digestif. Ordering a sparkling water with lime or some fruit juice and sparkling water combination, or creating the physical barrier of hand flat atop wine glass to signal abstention, elicited at least a friendly raised eyebrow if not a verbalized, "Pourquoi pas?" To which I had to decide whether to reply "Je ne bois pas ce soir" or "Je ne bois plus."

Although France has its share of abstainers from alcohol, from alcoholics to pregnant women to its significant Muslim population, the responses I received to my usual wine-decline seemed a touch more surprised than I had grown accustomed to in the States. *What's a nice girl like you doing not enjoying some of our best national product?* I imagined them saying with a beautiful accent. That perception could have been a projection on a people I longed to emulate from an early age, a sort of shame because I was unable to enjoy alcohol in moderation like my boyfriend. Surrounded by people seemingly enjoying wine and other alcohols normally, I wished I could have had just one glass.

Instead, during my trip to France and on that lonely night alone on the couch, I chose again to abstain from alcohol, to tolerate my discomfort, to remind myself to inhale and exhale and experience the full weight of my envy and urgency and desire. And I watched that desire to drink rise, abide, and eventually dissolve.

Each opportunity to drink—and they never go away—presents an opportunity for me to train in the concepts of impermanence and becoming more comfortable with discomfort. By choosing to sit with the unease, I have learned that the moment eventually passes.

By no means did I meditate away my desire to drink. Quite the contrary. But the space introduced by practicing meditation has also allowed me to see what I don't miss: the obsessing, the guilt and shame, the wasted time and opportunities, and the physical effects on my body and mind. Though I sometimes wish it were not so, the differences between my boyfriend's healthy relationship with alcohol and my abusive one are real. I continue to learn to sit with the knowledge that I'm different and the awareness that not drinking is one of the tradeoffs that comes as a result of being honest with myself.

CPSIA information can be obtained at www.ICGtesting.com
Printed in the USA
LVOW12s1926010216

473181LV00001B/202/P